# PUTTING GENDER ON THE AGENDA

## A Guide to Participating in UN World Conferences

**UNIFEM**
United Nations Development Fund For Women

**UN/NGLS**
United Nations Non-Governmental Liaison Service

The United Nations Development Fund for Women (UNIFEM) provides direct support for women's projects and promotes the inclusion of women in the decision-making processes of mainstream development programmes. UNIFEM's mission is to support efforts of women in the developing world to achieve their objective for economic and social development and for equality, and by so doing to improve the quality of life for all.

The United Nations Non-Governmental Liaison Service (UN-NGLS) is an inter-agency unit that specializes in development education and information work on North-South development issues and that facilitates dialogue and cooperation between development Non-governmental Organizations and the United Nations system. UN-NGLS has offices in Geneva and New York.

The views expressed in this handbook do not necessarily represent the views of UNIFEM, UN-NGLS, or the United Nations or any of its affiliated organizations.

©1995 UNIFEM
The United Nations Development Fund for Women
▶ 304 East 45th Street, New York, NY 10017, USA

UN-NGLS
United Nations Non-Governmental Liaison Service
▶ UN-NGLS, Palais des Nations, CH-1211 Geneva 10, Switzerland
▶ UN-NGLS, Rm. 6015, 866 UN Plaza, New York, NY 10017, USA

ISBN 0-912917-33-4

Cover and book design: ©Emerson, Wajdowicz Studios, Inc.,
1123 Broadway, New York, NY 10010, USA

Cover photo: ©Andrea Booher

Printed on Recycled Paper

# TABLE OF CONTENTS
▲▲▲▲

## Part 4: Working on a Conference at the National and Regional Levels

## Annexes

# ACKNOWLEDGEMENTS

▲▲▲▲

T he publication of this book has involved the creativity and commitment of many people who work with the United Nations (UN) in different capacities. All of their ideas and input have greatly enriched the final product, and the United Nations Development Fund for Women (UNIFEM) has benefited enormously from their time and energy.

The initial stages of conceptualizing this handbook involved Beti Astolfi of UNIFEM, Barbara Adams of the United Nations Non-Governmental Liaison Service (UN-NGLS) and Anne Walker of the International Women's Tribune Centre, in conjunction with Melanie Roth and Joanne Sandler of UNIFEM. As a result of their meetings, the outline and format of this book were widely field-tested among women's groups.

Barbara Adams produced the initial draft, which was then circulated for feedback among numerous development partners. The suggestions received from the Women's Environment and Development Organization (New York), Women, Law and Development (Harare), the World YWCA (Geneva), Status of Women Canada (Ottawa), and the UN Division for the Advancement of Women (New York) were particularly valuable. Colleagues at UNIFEM and UN-NGLS also commented on various drafts and made important contributions.

In addition to acknowledging the many individuals who contributed directly with comments and critiques, it is perhaps most important to acknowledge the work of thousands of women worldwide in breaking down barriers for NGO participation in intergovernmental meetings. It is our hope that this synthesis of what they have learned will ensure women's rightful place in international decision-making.

# PREFACE

▲▲▲▲

In 1975, International Women's Year, a world conference was held in Mexico City. This conference launched the UN Decade for Women, which was marked at its mid-point and conclusion by world conferences in Copenhagen and Nairobi respectively. In September 1995, China will host a Fourth World Conference on Women. These UN world conferences have been important catalysts and rallying cries in the struggle for women's rights.

Other UN world conferences have also attracted the attention and energy of women's organizations and other non-governmental organizations (NGOs). Recently, these have included the UN Conference on Environment and Development in 1992, the World Conference on Human Rights in 1993, the International Conference on Population and Development in 1994, and the World Summit for Social Development in 1995. NGO interest in influencing these conferences and their ability to do so has gained strength successively from conference to conference. This handbook has been written in recognition of this interest and in the hopes of contributing to the growing impact of NGO work in the intergovernmental arena.

To interact effectively with the international policy-setting and decision-making processes that UN world conferences represent, it is important to understand the relevant procedures and processes. The main purpose of this handbook is to provide specific and practical information about how these conferences work and how to enhance NGO participation. This handbook describes how UN world conferences are planned and organized and contains suggestions for NGO activities based on NGO experiences and enquiries.

This publication is a collaborative venture of the United Nations Development Fund for Women (UNIFEM) and the United Nations Non-Governmental Liaison Service (UN-NGLS). These organizations are actively involved in supporting NGO participation in the United Nations, but from different perspectives and with different constituencies and institutional responsibilities. The undertaking of this handbook has enabled them to pool their experiences and insights with a view to facilitating and strengthening the participation of women's organizations and other NGOs to advance an agenda for gender.

*Barbara Adams*

# BEFORE YOU BEGIN...

▲▲▲▲

This handbook was created to assist NGOs to

- ▶ make informed choices about whether to participate in UN world conferences
- ▶ determine what level of participation is most appropriate: national, regional, or international
- ▶ understand the requirements and procedures – both written and unwritten – for access to and effective participation of NGOs in UN world conferences
- ▶ undertake advance planning to improve NGO input into and participation at UN world conference activities.

Women who become involved in UN world conferences are making a decision to participate in global governance. They are staking out a sphere of influence over the setting of international priorities, efforts which ultimately affect national and local policy-making.

The process of setting and implementing policy is but one type of activity in which women advocates and organizers are involved. NGOs that are involved in women's issues and with many different communities of women – whether in direct service, advocacy, or other functions – must frequently make difficult choices about how to use the precious resources of time and money. So, before reading this book, it is useful to consider the following questions:

## How Does a UN World Conference Relate to Your Organizing Efforts?

For many women's organizations and advocates – whether working locally, nationally, or internationally – most UN meetings and their agendas appear to have little direct relevance. What impact will a UN world conference on population issues or human rights – held in a country on the other side of the world – have on the mobilizing, training, or advocacy work that is taking place in the cities and villages in which your organization is working? What impact will a UN world conference on human settlements have on your national health-advocacy work?

UN world conferences may be relevant to women's organizing activities for the following reasons, among others:

▶ Most of the countries in the world are members of the United Nations. These Member States make decisions and adopt resolutions at international meetings that carry implications and commitments for follow-up action in their own countries. The reports that your government prepares for UN world conferences and the commitments that your country's delegation makes are tools that can be used for national- and local-level organizing efforts.

▶ Most topics taken up at UN world conferences have a direct relation to local issues. These have included environment, human rights, population, education, and science and technology. Some UN world conferences have been designed specifically to put women and women's issues on the international agenda.

▶ Community groups can advocate at the local and national levels for the implementation of declarations and resolutions adopted at UN world conferences. For example, after a government signs the UN Convention on the Elimination of All Forms of Discrimination

Against Women (CEDAW), community groups can hold their government responsible for ratifying and implementing the terms of the agreement.

▶ What gets presented, debated, and agreed to at UN world conferences depends very much on how issues are framed. The input of people working at the local level on specific issues ensures that the UN debate reflects the realities that communities are facing. A UN world conference is an opportunity to say to your government, "These are the issues that we want you to take to this conference."

▶ Women's groups can benefit in a variety of ways from international solidarity and from building regional, multinational, and multicultural alliances. When women from different countries in the same region meet at a UN world conference, there is an opportunity to build a regional women's agenda. There are also opportunities to form international networks and alliances, which can become powerful sources of support and advocacy.

**Does Your Organization Want to Participate in a UN World Conference?**

Women's organizations may be interested in participating in UN world conferences for many reasons, including

▶ influencing government positions

▶ influencing the international community

▶ gathering information

▶ making contacts with other NGOs working in similar fields

▶ bringing international negotiations closer to individuals and local communities.

## AN EXAMPLE FROM THE UN WORLD CONFERENCE ON HUMAN RIGHTS

In 1991, women from 20 countries participated in a meeting on women's human rights sponsored by the Center for Women's Global Leadership. At the meeting, it was decided that the UN World Conference on Human Rights in 1993 would provide an opportunity to mobilize and focus on women's rights. The women initiated a petition, calling upon the Conference to "comprehensively address women's human rights at every level of its proceedings" and to recognize gender violence as "a violation of human rights requiring immediate action."

They agreed on the language of the petition and began a campaign to gather signatures. Some organized hearings on women's human rights in order to educate others.

Using women's alternative media networks, the original 20 women were able to spread news about the petition to many other countries. The result was a petition that was co-sponsored by over 300 women's organizations.

The impact was both international and local. At the international level, a petition with 500,000 signatures from 124 countries was presented to the World Conference on Human Rights. Locally, the petition became an excellent tool around which to organize and raise awareness about women's rights.

You may participate in a UN world conference in many different ways: you may participate without leaving home, you may participate as part of a large coalition, you may participate in the preparations or in the implementation of conference results.

This book will provide information that you can use to make some of these choices and to ensure that your participation is effective.

In addition to the official UN world conference, an NGO Forum is frequently organized which has an agenda separate from the official UN world conference and includes workshops, networking and information-gathering opportunities. This book focuses on the process of participating in a UN world conference.

# UNITED NATIONS WORLD CONFERENCES: SETTING A GLOBAL AGENDA

▲▲▲▲

# SETTING A GLOBAL AGENDA
▲▲▲▲

ince the establishment of the United Nations in 1945, numerous world conferences have taken place on such diverse subjects as disarmament, population policy, and human settlements. While the process for convening these conferences and for agreeing on the governmental commitments that they produce has evolved over the years, there are some common characteristics for all.

## CONVENING A UN WORLD CONFERENCE

▶ **WHEN**  Conferences are convened when the international community agrees that the policy direction of an important issue needs to be reassessed, updated, or given special attention.

▶ **HOW**  Preparing for UN world conferences usually requires a minimum of two years during which the agenda, objectives, and scope of the conferences and their outcomes are determined by Member States of the United Nations. This process frequently involves national- and regional-level meetings, expert group meetings, data gathering, and drafting position papers, which are fed into the global discussions.

▶ **WHY**  The conferences vary in purpose, but the objective of most is to produce an internationally agreed-upon statement of principles and standards, and an action plan for implementation. This often involves policy changes and commitments by governments and provides direction for the work of the United Nations.

# SETTING A WOMEN'S AGENDA
▲▲▲▲

The three world conferences of the UN Decade for Women – held in 1975 (Mexico City), 1980 (Copenhagen), and 1985 (Nairobi) – were important mobilizing and awareness-raising events. The Decade resulted in a consensus document, *Nairobi Forward-Looking Strategies for the Advancement of Women to the Year 2000 (FLS)*. This document contains a comprehensive set of strategies for advancing the status of women worldwide.

These conferences made women more aware of the valuable opportunities for organizing locally, nationally, regionally, and internationally, and for influencing policy-making.

Recently, women's NGOs have begun to organize coalitions and petitions, undertake research, circulate position papers, and work collaboratively with national governments in preparing for and during UN world conferences that do not have women as a specific theme. Women are increasingly making an effort to attend and to find ways to influence these conferences. Their efforts are yielding results.

## PUTTING WOMEN ON THE AGENDA AT THE UNITED NATIONS CONFERENCE ON ENVIRONMENT AND DEVELOPMENT (UNCED)
### Rio de Janeiro, 1992

A number of activities throughout the preparatory process positioned women's NGOs to play a large role in UNCED:

NGO participation in the preparatory meetings enabled NGOs to mobilize for action. This resulted in women building alliances with each other and with governments and UN agencies to influence the Conference agenda. The women's caucus, which grew out of this alliance-building, contributed to the decision on "Women, Environment and Development," which was unanimously adopted by Member States.

This landmark decision requested that "key elements relating to women's critical economic, social and environmental contributions to sustainable development be addressed ... in all the substantive documentation, particularly *Agenda 21*, the Earth Charter and the Conventions." It further requested that "recommendations from relevant meetings held by governments, intergovernmental and non-governmental organizations be made available to the Preparatory Committee." This enabled the recommendations from key NGO initiatives to be integrated into UNCED documentation and, in particular, Chapter 24 of *Agenda 21*, "Global Action for Women Towards Sustainable and Equitable Development."

The 1991 United Nations Environmental Programme (UNEP) meeting, Global Assembly – Partners in Life, showcased 218 success stories of women's roles in environmental management. The World Congress for a Healthy Planet, sponsored by the Women's Environment and Development Organization (WEDO), was attended by 1,500 women (from 84 nations) who reached consensus on a *Women's Action Agenda 21*. Both meetings contributed to the preparations for UNCED.

This UNCED example of strengthening partnerships between governments, the United Nations, and NGOs illustrates a way to incorporate the gender dimension into international decision-making.

# THE PARTICIPANTS
▲▲▲▲

The United Nations is an international body with a
membership of more than 180 Member States.
Governments determine whether to hold a UN world
conference and which issues they will address. They are
the only voting members at UN world conferences and
their preparatory meetings.

**Governments**

The size and composition of government delegations can
vary greatly. In general, delegations include senior ministry
representatives, technical experts, representatives from
the mission or embassy where the meeting is held, and,
increasingly, NGO representatives. It is important to note,
however, that governments are not required to include
NGOs on their delegations.

**UN Agencies,
Programmes,
and Funds**

Various UN bodies contribute to the preparations of UN
world conferences and monitor the implementation of
conference results. They may also be responsible for
implementing selected recommendations. They do not,
however, vote at the conferences and cannot enforce
resolutions that result from the meetings.

**NGOs**

NGOs are increasingly important actors at UN world
conferences. Although NGOs do not have an official
negotiating role or the right to vote, they do have a variety
of opportunities to influence UN deliberations. These are
discussed at greater length in Part 3.

**The United
Nations
Conference
Secretariat**

A Conference Secretariat is specifically established to service
and administer a UN world conference. A special secretariat may be set up or the task may be given to an existing
part of the UN Secretariat. The head of the Conference
Secretariat is usually called the "Secretary-General."

The responsibilities of the Conference Secretariat include:

▶ preparing background and substantive documents

▶ preparing questionnaires that can serve as a basis for national reports submitted by Member States and collating national and regional information and data

▶ convening expert-group meetings

▶ compiling a draft programme of action

▶ overseeing publication of a regular newsletter providing updated information on conference-planning activities

▶ making available copies of official documents

▶ providing information on the status of national and regional reports

▶ servicing and facilitating negotiations between governments

▶ accrediting NGOs.

## DOES THE CONFERENCE SECRETARIAT HAVE A WOMEN'S ADVISOR?

The appointment of a Special Advisor on Women to the Conference Secretariat for UNCED was important for a variety of reasons, including the access to the official process that it provided for women's NGOs. The Special Advisor on Women promoted awareness of gender issues among Conference Secretariat staff and monitored all preparatory documents for their gender sensitivity.

The Special Advisor on Women helped NGOs to understand the conference process and found ways to convey NGO experiences and concerns to Conference Secretariat staff and official delegates. She formulated a questionnaire on women's roles in environment and development, the results of which were included in the national reports submitted by Member States.

# THE PROCESS FROM THE INITIAL IDEA TO THE UN WORLD CONFERENCE

▲▲▲

# ANATOMY OF A UN WORLD CONFERENCE
▲▲▲▲

**W**hile there are some variations, most UN world conferences go through a series of steps over a two- or three-year period. Below is an overview of the stages that are common to the convening of UN world conferences:

▶ The UN General Assembly (GA) or the UN Economic and Social Council (ECOSOC) passes a resolution that calls on Member States and the United Nations to hold the conference and also outlines the goals, agenda, and the preparatory process.

▶ A Conference Secretariat is set up. Among other functions, it prepares UN documentation which is circulated to governments in all official UN languages.

▶ National governments decide on their own policies and positions, prepare reports, convene delegations, and participate in intergovernmental regional meetings prior to attending the conference.

▶ A Preparatory Committee (PrepCom) is formed, which will hold a series of meetings at which Member States develop an agenda and programme of work for the conference. It also negotiates most of the content of the major documents and outcomes of the conference at these preparatory meetings.

▶ Expert group meetings on the priority areas of the conference deepen the treatment of complex issues and provide recommendations to the PrepCom and the conference. For some UN world conferences, the Conference Secretariat convenes — or asks other groups to convene — expert group meetings.

## PREPARING AT THE NATIONAL LEVEL

What happens at the national level significantly influences the outcome of a UN world conference. Countries may be involved in a variety of activities in preparation for their participation in a UN world conference. For instance, they may

▶ *Prepare reports and collect data on issues related to the subject of the conference.* Sometimes, a questionnaire is circulated to national governments by the Conference Secretariat asking for specific information about the current status of related issues, or about progress made since a previous world conference. In other instances, governments are asked to prepare national reports on the conference topic according to a specific format and including certain types of information. The process that is used to respond to these questionnaires or prepare these reports can have a significant impact on their content.

▶ *Select members of delegations to the conference and preparatory-committee meetings and regional preparatory meetings.* It is the responsibility of the delegations to present their country's policies in the conference process. Delegations vary significantly with regard to the extent of knowledge that delegation members have on the topic, the extent to which a diverse range of experience is represented, and the autonomy that delegations have to make decisions. They also vary in size, with some consisting of only three or four people and others with as many as 80 members.

▶ *Hold meetings or consultations related to topics to be discussed at the UN world conference.*

▶ Intergovernmental regional meetings are organized to formulate a common approach and set regional priorities. (See Annex 2 for a listing of the Regional Economic Commissions). The impact that regional meetings will have on the preparatory process for a UN world conference varies. In some instances, the regional meetings provide critical opportunities for governments to gather and develop regional positions. There are UN world conferences, however, for which there may be no significant regional gathering.

▶ The UN world conference takes place, negotiations initiated at the PrepComs are completed, and final documents are adopted, usually by consensus among Member States.

▶ Follow-up to the decisions made at the conference can include national, regional, and international implementation, monitoring, and review. This longer-term process provides the framework for measuring the accountability of governments in fulfilling commitments made at the conference and of the UN system in carrying out the recommended programme of work.

# PREPARATORY COMMITTEE MEETINGS

▲▲▲▲

At least 60 percent of the final outcome of a UN world conference is determined during the preparatory process. By the time the official delegations gather at the site of a UN world conference, the positions, agreements, and disagreements have been discussed and debated.

The preparatory process is the period during which those involved try to build commitment to the agreements being sought. It is also the key time for NGOs to become officially accredited to the conference and its PrepCom and to identify other NGOs that are active on the issues of the conference. (See page 22 for information on accreditation.)

Throughout the preparatory process, the Conference Secretariat manages the process of drafting and re-drafting working documents and action plans and incorporating changes and agreements as they are decided by Member States. Any item or language that has not been agreed to by the time the UN world conference is held appears in bracketed text in the conference documents.

NGOs and women's organizations have traditionally concentrated their attention and resources on attending the UN world conference itself and on their own parallel activities. However, there is a growing interest in influencing the outcome of the official conferences by becoming involved in the preparatory process and in the regional meetings when these are scheduled.

The following section provides specific information on the structure and organization of the PrepCom and on the process of negotiation that takes place in PrepCom meetings.

# THE PREPCOM PROCESS
▲▲▲▲

The PrepCom for a UN world conference is organized in the same way as the conference. It is composed of representatives of governments and is serviced by the Conference Secretariat.

Up to four PrepCom meetings can be held prior to a UN world conference. Sessions of a PrepCom take from one to four weeks each and are usually held at one of the UN locations, primarily New York or Geneva.

The major task of a PrepCom is to initiate negotiations towards the adoption of the final documents.

The first substantive session of the PrepCom has the task of determining the basic elements and hence the scope of the final outcome of the conference. Some progress will also be made on the structure and form of the final documents, be they a declaration, a set of principles, or a plan of action.

The PrepCom directly preceding the UN World Conference will be dominated by negotiations between Member States on the issues. Delegates will receive draft copies of the final documents. Passages that are square bracketed (denoted by [ ]) are those to which one or more delegations have objected, and the negotiations will focus, for the most part, on resolving disagreement in those areas. If consensus is not reached on specific items or language, these square brackets may remain in the document, indicating certain governments' objections to the text.

# REACHING CONSENSUS: NEGOTIATING THE OUTCOME OF A UN WORLD CONFERENCE

▲▲▲▲

The decision-making process, from the general debate through the working and informal groups, consists of various methods to reach consensus. This takes the form of protracted negotiations and compromises to reach decisions and resolutions that will be contained in a report to be adopted at the conclusion of the meeting. The aim of the negotiations is to draft a text that all governments will adopt by consensus.

**Conference Document**

There are different kinds of documents, agreements, resolutions, and decisions, which can all be part of the outcome or process of a major conference. The final documents that emerge from the conference process are generally composed of

- ▶ a **declaration**, or a general statement of principles, which serves to set the moral tone and political imperative of the issue

- ▶ a **programme of action**, a prescriptive outline, or blueprint of steps that governments have agreed should be taken at the national, regional, and international levels

- ▶ the **means of implementation**, which include funding needs and institutional measures, are sometimes the last chapter or last section of every chapter of a programme of action. This section specifies mechanisms for putting recommendations into action, and is an important part of the document that NGOs can use for future monitoring and accountability.

Understanding the importance of these documents and how to use them after the conference is useful for NGOs.

**Negotiating Process**

Finding a way to influence what is included in these documents is a particular challenge. The following is a rough description of the different phases of a typical negotiating process for PrepComs and UN world conferences alike:

▶ Delegates to the conference select a chairperson, vice-chairpersons, and rapporteur, and formally adopt the agenda.

▶ The plenary session usually begins with a general debate which contains statements from governments and UN agencies. Government statements articulate the national position and priorities and serve to place official policy on the record. NGOs also have opportunities to make statements.

▶ Sometimes a group or coalition of governments makes a joint statement.

▶ Draft texts are prepared and sponsored by governments or groupings of governments. The outline of a programme of action and the initial drafts are often prepared for government deliberations by the Conference Secretariat.

▶ The draft text become the focus of discussion and reaction, usually in an "informal" session (a session closed to the press and for which there is no official record).

▶ Working groups are formed to undertake negotiations which include specific amendments proposed by government delegates.

## GOVERNMENT NEGOTIATING GROUPS

Below are some of the groupings of governments as of 1993 that have evolved within the UN system. Some of these groups are well established in the UN system, such as the Group of 77 (G-77). Others, such as the European Union, are formal institutions both within and outside the UN system, while others have developed more recently.

▶ **Arab Maghreb Union:** Algeria, Libya, Mauritania, Morocco, Tunisia

▶ **CANZ:** Canada, Australia, New Zealand

▶ **CARICOM [Caribbean Community]:** Antigua & Barbuda, Bahamas, Barbados, Belize, Dominica, Grenada, Guyana, Jamaica, Saint Kitts & Nevis, Saint Lucia, Saint Vincent & the Grenadines, Trinidad & Tobago

▶ **Eastern and Central Europe**\*

▶ **European Union:** Belgium, Denmark, France, Germany, Greece, Ireland, Italy, Luxembourg, Netherlands, Portugal, Spain, United Kingdom

▶ **G-77:** Caucus of 132 developing countries

▶ **NORDICS:** Denmark, Finland, Iceland, Norway, Sweden

\*The status of this group is unclear since the collapse of the Eastern bloc.

**2**

▶ If the amendments do not command agreement from all the negotiators, they are placed in square brackets, meaning that further discussion and amendment are required.

▶ Once negotiations have taken place and consensus has been reached among Member States, the brackets are removed and the text can no longer be changed at any stage of the process. Future work is concentrated on square bracketed language upon which consensus has not yet been reached.

▶ On particularly controversial issues, the chairperson might ask a smaller number of governments that disagree on particular language to caucus, settle their differences, and come back to the meeting with agreed-upon language.

▶ At various stages during this process, different techniques and types of papers are used to facilitate negotiations among governments. These include the chairperson's summaries, non-papers, conference-room papers and other papers. Governments sometimes try to change the draft altogether in midstream and present their own versions, which may or may not be accepted as the new basis for negotiations.

▶ As the pace of negotiations picks up, new draft paragraphs can be issued on an almost hourly basis. They are identified by date/time only, and are generally available only in English.

▶ While negotiations take place in the PrepCom, diplomats frequently and regularly consult with their relevant national ministry. The ministry decides how to respond – whether to adjust the policy and write the changes into its plans, whether to accept proposed formulations or offer alternative suggestions – and when and how far to compromise.

▶ Generally, as the conference conclusion nears, the group meetings of delegates become smaller. Chairpersons or convenors of negotiating groups may hold informal discussions in small conference rooms, their offices, in the corridor, or "over coffee." Such meetings are, of course, not listed in the *UN Journal,* which announces daily meetings.

▶ Eventually, text will be issued with all the newly agreed-upon language incorporated into the draft, including any remaining square brackets, which will reveal a great deal about which areas of disagreement are the most contentious (although not necessarily *why* they are).

▶ Negotiations will continue until consensus is reached or a vote is taken on the resolution or decision. In the final stages of a session, negotiations frequently go late into the night.

▶ A text is rarely "defeated" by vote, as the sponsors will usually withdraw the text if they are not sure of a majority. Only in the rarest of cases, if ever, will a major programme of action be put to a vote. Consensus is the rule.

▶ Finally, the chairperson will hold a press conference to announce the results to the media.

# NGO ACTIVITIES AND STRATEGIES TO INFLUENCE THE NEGOTIATING PROCESS

▲▲▲▲

3

# PREPARING TO ATTEND THE CONFERENCE OR PREPCOM

▲▲▲▲

**NGO Accreditation to UN World Conferences**

To be able to participate in UN world conferences or their preparatory meetings, NGOs need to become accredited. Once accredited, NGOs receive

▶ a grounds pass to enter the buildings where the UN conferences are being held

▶ access to documents

▶ access to the main conference rooms where governments meet

▶ the opportunity to deliver oral and written statements

▶ the opportunity to discuss issues and positions with relevant delegates, other NGOs, and staff.

**NGOs in consultative status** * with ECOSOC are usually eligible to participate in all UN world conferences. They must, however, indicate their interest in doing so by writing to the appropriate Conference Secretariat.

**NGOs without consultative status** can become accredited to participate in a specific conference or PrepCom by writing to the Conference Secretariat for an accreditation application form. The application process usually requires the following information:

▶ copies of the latest annual report and most recent budget

---

*Consultative status with ECOSOC allows NGOs limited access to UN documentation, meetings, and services. To obtain information about consultative status, write to: NGO Unit/DPCSD, 2 UN Plaza, Room 2340 New York, NY 10017, USA.

> ▶ copies of constitution by-laws and information on governing-body composition
> ▶ proof of the non-profit nature of the organization
> ▶ a short statement of how the organization's activities relate to the conference, a description of membership, and location of headquarters.

For international meetings, NGOs should write to the appropriate Conference Secretariat for application information. For regional meetings, accreditation is usually obtained through the Regional Economic Commissions in a separate but similar process. (See Annex 2 for addresses of Regional Economic Commissions.)

Guidelines and criteria for NGO participation in UN world conferences are determined by the General Assembly or ECOSOC. It is important to apply for accreditation as early as possible, keep current on any changing situations, and inquire about procedures well in advance.

# A CHECKLIST
▲▲▲▲

✓ Think about your "on-site" strategy ahead of time. For instance, you should

> ▶ define what you want to achieve at the meeting
> ▶ be aware that many aspects important to you may not be explicitly on the UN agenda
> ▶ be well-informed about the agenda and the issues of the conference.

✓ Think strategically about who should attend and how many representatives your organization might send.

▶ Who in your organization has relevant experience and is interested in attending these types of conferences?

▶ Who will be best at lobbying, participating in caucuses and coalitions, and representing your organization's interests?

▶ Are there other organizations from your area that are sending representatives with whom you can work?

▶ Can a number of organizations work together to raise funds for one person to attend and represent all?

✓ Your organization needs to become "accredited" in advance to observe official sessions at UN world conferences or their preparatory meetings. Contact the Conference Secretariat or speak with other individuals in your organization to find out if your group has accreditation. Each conference has its own deadlines for accreditation.

✓ Bring proof of your accreditation and personal identification.

✓ Collect the meeting documentation that is available in advance. Use UN and NGO materials as a way of finding out the international dimensions of the issues.

✓ Some meeting documentation can be sent to you by the Conference Secretariat, and it is increasingly available on electronic communication networks. Have your name placed on the mailing list of the Conference Secretariat as well as with other organizations that regularly provide conference information.

✓ Contact other NGOs working nationally, regionally, and internationally about their priorities and preparations. Joint preparation with NGOs in the region often helps to generate political momentum, add impact to your statements, and avoid unnecessary duplication of work.

✓ Cooperate with NGOs that are working on the same issues but will not be able to travel to the conference or preparatory meetings. Being physically present at an intergovernmental meeting is not the only effective way to influence a UN world conference. Much of the national-level work (see Part 4) can be carried out very effectively through networking and information sharing.

✓ Prepare position papers. These are very useful conference tools. Keep them short – only a few pages if possible. Each paper should clearly state your proposals for action by governments and the UN system.

✓ Send your position papers to the relevant government departments, other NGOs, both in your region and elsewhere, and to the Conference Secretariat. NGOs are increasingly using electronic communication networks to disseminate their position papers.

✓ Work with the media activities can help mobilize public support for your views and encourage governments to accept them. Media activities (press releases, contact with journalists, etc.) should be integrated into your conference preparation.

✓ When attending a UN world conference or PrepCom, plan to stay at least 24 hours beyond the official end of the meeting, as they frequently run late.

✓ Arrive one day before the meeting starts (longer if you have trouble with jet lag). Frequently, there are NGO planning meetings or an NGO orientation session.

✓ Bring a portable office to the meeting.

On-site facilities and computer access have sometimes been made available to NGOs at recent PrepComs and conferences. However, unless your organization or group has made special arrangements in advance, it is unlikely that copying and office facilities will be easily available.

✓ Some items to bring with you are:

> ▶ a letter from your organization stating that you are the organization's representative, to satisfy the accreditation procedures when you register
>
> ▶ a passport or some other identification to be used for the issuing of a UN grounds pass
>
> ▶ copies of your position papers (in all UN languages if possible) for distribution
>
> ▶ stationery/letterhead with your organization's name, address, phone/fax number, and other important information on it
>
> ▶ business cards
>
> ▶ general information on the work of your organization.

# WORKING WITH GOVERNMENT DELEGATES

▲▲▲▲

A t all UN meetings – whether international or regional – influencing the outcomes depends upon the ability of NGOs to identify government delegates who are sympathetic to their views and willing to work collaboratively. It is also important to identify and interact with delegates who have views very different from your own. In working with delegates, it is important to keep the following in mind:

▶ Some delegates are highly qualified experts in their fields or skilled negotiators from a country's diplomatic service, while others might be attending the international meeting for the first time. Some delegates are used to working closely with NGOs, while others have little or no experience of doing so.

▶ The beginning and end of daily sessions are a good time to interact with delegates.

▶ Delegates can be identified by noting the country sign at their seat.

▶ Some social functions, receptions, lunches, coffee breaks, etc., can provide a good opportunity to talk to delegates informally.

▶ Delegates are often willing to use NGO proposals if these are presented in UN style.

▶ If delegates include your concerns or take up your suggested amendments in their positions, do not forget to express your appreciation.

## WORKING WITH DELEGATES AT PREPCOM III FOR THE UN INTERNATIONAL CONFERENCE ON POPULATION AND DEVELOPMENT (ICPD)

Held in New York in April 1994, PrepCom III for the ICPD focused on the most recent draft of the final conference document. At previous PrepCom meetings, the women's caucus had worked with delegates to ensure that the draft document incorporated women's concerns throughout the chapters and to secure inclusion of a chapter specifically on women.

At PrepCom III, a crucial recommendation contained in Chapter 15 came under discussion. The passage being debated specified that governments should work in partnership with NGOs. Some dissenting delegates preferred a recommendation that governments should "cooperate" with NGOs, rather than work in partnership.

Women from NGOs who were attending PrepCom III – including those from the countries that were opposing the wording of the recommendation – mobilized further discussion on this issue through regional caucuses and the women's caucus. They held meetings with delegates to encourage dialogue and to gain an understanding of the objections that the delegates were raising. Using information gathered during these meetings, the women's caucus organized a general discussion to which they invited all delegates.

A full discussion of concerns and priorities by all parties resulted in greater understanding and agreement. The delegates withdrew their objections, and the recommendation that governments work in partnership with NGOs remained.

# WORKING WITH OTHER NGOS

▲▲▲▲

Working with other NGOs – and, specifically, with women's NGOs and caucuses – is one of the most important strategies for influencing an international or regional UN meeting. Even NGOs that disagree about certain approaches and priorities may find areas of common interest and be able to work together to include their concerns on the agenda.

As an NGO representative at an international or regional meeting, you could consider the following:

▸ There is frequently an NGO meeting room. Find out where this is and visit frequently to obtain up-to-date information.

▸ Meet regularly with NGOs to exchange information. By working with others, you can cover multiple simultaneous meetings, help each other monitor government positions, and coordinate lobbying efforts.

▸ Find NGOs from your country and organize together to hold a meeting with your government delegation. You can also arrange briefings open to all NGOs to attend.

▸ Share official conference documents, which are frequently in short supply or less readily available to NGOs.

▸ Circulate useful NGO statements and materials widely to the Conference Secretariat, Member State delegations, and other NGOs.

▸ Organize with NGOs from your region into regional caucuses or organize around specific issue or thematic areas. You can develop common strategies, prepare statements, and suggest amendments to government negotiating texts.

**3**

▶ At UN world conferences and preparatory meetings, NGOs often organize to produce a daily newspaper. This is usually an excellent source of information and opinions. You might contribute an article to it or have your position paper printed.

# WORKING THROUGH A CAUCUS
▲▲▲▲

A t many UN meetings, NGOs, and sometimes UN delegates and staff, form caucuses or groups of organizations and individuals interested in similar issues. Caucuses meet regularly (often daily) to exchange information, hold briefings, and formulate positions or statements relevant to the conference proceedings. The caucus can also meet with policy makers who will be responsible for implementing the programme of action produced by the conference.

Often at UN world conferences, women join together to form a women's caucus. Many times, the women's caucus has worked successfully to ensure that the priorities of women become part of the negotiations.

In addition, caucuses are often formed around a wide range of issues covered by a given conference agenda and on a regional basis.

**INSIDE THE WOMEN'S CAUCUS
AT THE WORLD CONFERENCE ON HUMAN RIGHTS (WCHR)
Vienna, 1993**

The women's caucus at the WCHR was organized to promote dialogue between members of UN agencies, official government delegates, the press, and others attending the conference.

During the first week, the caucus met daily to strategize about how to incorporate women's concerns into the draft declaration. Recommendations made by women's groups, who held a separate caucus, were used as a basis for discussions. The dialogue between NGOs and official delegates was crucial to ensuring that the women's recommendations were incorporated into the final document, since the drafting committee was closed to NGOs.

In the second week, the caucus shifted its focus to the implementation of the paragraphs already incorporated into the document. The caucus met with key players responsible for the follow-up to the WCHR. These included representatives of UN human rights treaty-monitoring bodies (the committees set up to supervise the implementation of the human-rights conventions), special rapporteurs, and the staff of the UN Centre for Human Rights responsible for carrying out the Vienna Declaration. The caucus asked these representatives to discuss and share their thoughts on how they would concretely address the gender components in their implementation steps.

After the conference ended many of the networks formed through the women's caucus continued. Women's groups are working closely with the UN Centre for Human Rights to assist them in monitoring and addressing acts of gender violence. Government officials concerned with women's issues are now in close contact with NGOs working in this area.

**3**

# WORKING WITH THE SECRETARIAT
▲▲▲▲

The Conference Secretariat plays an important role in the conference process: the Conference Secretariat prepares the background documents for a conference, drafts programmes, and may be involved in implementing the results of a conference. The Conference Secretariat is *not* the decision-making body for a conference – only governments ultimately make the decisions – but information on the issues provided by the Conference Secretariat can be a valuable component informing the process. The inclusion of contributions from NGOs in the documentation related to conferences is becoming more common, but there is no established procedure for doing this.

The Conference Secretariat usually assigns at least one officer to work with NGOs. This person will answer enquiries from NGOs and keep them informed on conference developments.

Working with the Conference Secretariat can include the following:

▸ Establish contact with the Conference Secretariat staff responsible for information and liaison with NGOs.

▸ Identify secretariat programme staff who are writing reports on substantive issues, and enquire about how to submit useful and relevant information.

▸ Tailor your material according to the mandate of the conference. The Conference Secretariat usually appreciates substantive contributions and concrete suggestions – especially if brief, accurate, and to the point.

# MAKING STATEMENTS AT UN WORLD CONFERENCES
▲▲▲▲

**N**GOs accredited to the UN world conference can make statements by requesting a place on the speaker's list, which is handled by the Conference Secretariat.

If you are going to make a statement:

▶ Keep it brief and to the point. Be polite, but make your points clearly. If the meeting has interpretation, speak slowly enough for the interpreters to keep up with you. If there is a time limit for statements, keep within it.

▶ Avoid general statements. Be relevant to the agenda item. Aim for concrete proposals for action.

▶ Have written copies of your statement available for delegates, interpreters, and the Conference Secretariat.

▶ Think strategically about the pros and cons of making a statement. You can often approach delegates individually.

▶ NGOs often present joint statements at meetings or circulate joint position papers. These can have an influence on the negotiations and are a way for NGOs to express their solidarity.

▶ When presenting any statement, joint or otherwise, do not say that you are speaking on behalf of all the NGOs at the meeting unless you are sure that every NGO at the meeting supports your statement.

**3**

# WORKING WITH THE MEDIA
▲▲▲▲

taff of the mass media which includes journalists from nationally and internationally circulated newspapers, television, and radio – as well as representatives from the "alternative" media – attend UN world conferences.

▶ Media activities (press releases, contacts with journalists) could be integrated into your organization's overall strategy for attending the conference and mobilizing public support for your positions.

▶ At the meeting itself, ask the Conference Secretariat for a list of "accredited correspondents." Note those from your own country (or international media) and introduce yourself to them. Provide them with information, positions and commentary.

---

### THE UNITED NATIONS DEPARTMENT OF PUBLIC INFORMATION (DPI)

At UN world conferences, DPI coordinates the UN relationship with the press (newspapers, radio, television, etc.). This involves organizing a press room, holding daily briefings, distributing press releases, and sponsoring press conferences and other events.

If you qualify, you could become accredited to DPI prior to the conference. This ensures access to information and resources, including press-room facilities.

For additional information, write to:

Media Accreditation and Liaison Unit, S-0250 Department of Public Information, United Nations, New York, NY 10017, USA.

# WORKING ON A CONFERENCE AT THE NATIONAL AND REGIONAL LEVELS

▲▲▲▲

# IDEAS FOR NGOS WORKING AT THE NATIONAL LEVEL

▲▲▲▲

Much can be done even without being physically present in the meeting of a PrepCom or a conference of the UN. In fact, it could even be said that the work at the international level counts for little without corresponding and complementary work at the national (and local) level.

Here are some ideas on what can be done at the national level:

▶ Identify the government ministries and staff preparing your government's position. Suggest consultations as they prepare their reports, responses and recommendations.

▶ Find out who will be on your national delegation to the regional and international preparatory meetings and the UN world conference. Establish contact with them.

▶ Set up meetings with government representatives before they attend UN world conferences in order to have input into the policy-formulation process and national reports. Provide them with your own data, studies, or position papers.

▶ Prepare information on the upcoming conference in order to mobilize awareness among your country's citizens. Try to convince the local press to cover stories about the meeting, its importance, and your government's participation.

▶ Encourage gender balance and participation of NGOs on the delegation.

- ▶ Enquire about and seek input into the government's responses to the questionnaires sent by the Conference Secretariat to solicit governments' views. National responses are usually coordinated domestically by the foreign or relevant ministry.

- ▶ Link up with other organizations to achieve greater influence.

- ▶ Work with parliamentarians who can monitor government preparations and provide information on issues being debated. Where feasible, arrange for parliamentary discussions on your government's policies.

- ▶ Ask for copies of your government's UN statements. These are public documents and available from foreign ministries and UN Missions. Addresses of UN Missions can be obtained from the foreign ministry in your country.

4

# THE REGIONAL PREPARATORY PROCESS FOR UN CONFERENCES
▲▲▲▲

To influence the regional process

- ▶ establish contact with the relevant Regional Economic Commission (see Annex 2)
- ▶ work with groups at the national level before the regional preparatory meeting; if possible, develop a regional NGO position or programme for the conference
- ▶ explore the possibilities for having NGO and women's organization representatives appointed to your national delegation in the regional meeting
- ▶ organize or participate in a women's caucus and other relevant meetings.

# EXPERT-GROUP MEETINGS AND SPECIFIC-ISSUE REPORTS
▲▲▲▲

Many UN world conferences will include expert-group meetings on the particular conference issues as part of their preparatory process.

Opportunities exist for NGOs to influence the outcomes of expert-group meetings and the resulting recommendations. Contact the Conference Secretariat to find out the schedule of meetings and the opportunities for NGOs to contribute and attend.

## USING AN EXPERT-GROUP MEETING TO PUT YOUR ISSUES ON THE AGENDA

At the request of the Secretary General for the Fourth World Conference on Women (WCW), UNIFEM convened a three-day expert-group meeting entitled "Women, Science and Technology: New Visions for the 21st Century" in December 1993. The meeting was attended by 55 participants from governments, NGOs, science and technology institutions, academia and UN agencies.

The expert group was convened to develop a set of recommendations to ensure that women play a substantive role in reorienting the philosophy and practice of science and technology to emphasize basic human needs. Background papers were prepared and submitted by various participants, reflecting their experiences and perspectives in incorporating gender considerations in national, regional, and international science and technology activities. Working groups to review and discuss the papers were formed around a number of science and technology topics. Each working group developed recommendations, which were discussed and refined in the plenary.

To increase the impact of its work and ensure that its recommendations would continue to be pressed at activities related to the WCW, the expert-group meeting was planned as part of a series of related gatherings. It was held in conjunction with the Commission on Science and Technology for Development. The meeting was followed by a convening of members of the Once and Future Consortium, a network of agencies and NGOs dedicated to "re-envisioning women, science and technology towards 1995 and beyond." A report of the meeting was also widely circulated to NGOs, relevant government ministries, science and technology institutions, academics, and people interested in ensuring greater gender equity in science and technology development.

A final set of *Recommendations for Action* were submitted by the expert group for consideration in the formulation of the WCW's *Platform for Action*.

4

# BEYOND THE CONFERENCE
▲▲▲▲

T he results of a UN world conference extend beyond whatever final document or plan it produces. The final documents will specify mechanisms for follow-up, monitoring, and accountability. These elements become the basis upon which longer-term actions and strategies can be formulated.

The more far-reaching "chain" of outcomes resulting from a UN world conference include the following:

► The political process in which governments have engaged results in highlighting or reaffirming a new set of international priorities.

► Additionally, consideration needs to be undertaken about the organizations, infrastructure and financing – at the international level, as well as regionally and nationally – that will be involved in meeting these priorities.

The funding and institutional arrangements that are undertaken as follow-up – or that are pledged but may receive little attention in the aftermath of the conference – are also areas in which NGO input is critical. Agreements that are not implemented can undermine the credibility of the process and of the players.

To monitor the commitments that governments have made, it is important to remember these points:

► The documents that result from UN world conferences are written in formal legislative language, and their contents result from political negotiation and compromise. They may not be the most elegant, inspiring prose, but they may still be of use to women and women's groups working for social change worldwide.

▶ UN resolutions and recommendations are but the first step in the process of achieving the aims that they express. The central importance of these resolutions lies in the follow-up undertaken by Member States.

▶ UN resolutions and recommendations are not legally binding. Signing or endorsing the programme of action or series of resolutions is not equivalent to passing legislation. A programme of action is effective when it is used as a guide for national legislation, or when it helps shape international priorities in the future.

▶ UN resolutions and recommendations are addressed to different bodies. Many of the final documents or programmes of action resulting from UN world conferences contain recommendations to governments, to the UN system, to NGOs, and to other specific types of institutions.

▶ UN resolutions and recommendations generally specify an international agency or institution that is responsible for monitoring progress achieved in fulfilling agreed-upon resolutions. For instance, the Commission on the Status of Women was named as the agency responsible for monitoring and reporting to the United Nations on progress made in fulfilling the resolutions and recommendations contained in the *Nairobi Forward-Looking Strategies for the Advancement of Women to the Year 2000.*

## USING THE *NAIROBI FORWARD-LOOKING STRATEGIES FOR THE ADVANCEMENT OF WOMEN TO THE YEAR 2000 (FLS)*

The *FLS* document that emerged from the World Conference to Review and Appraise the Achievements of the UN Decade for Women (Nairobi, 1985) was intended to provide a blueprint for action to advance the status of women in national and international economic, social, cultural, and legal development to the year 2000. Each of its sections identifies obstacles to progress, basic strategies to overcome obstacles, and specific measures to implement strategies. It was a document that interested groups could use to pressure for action. Below are examples of two attempts.

▶ A GOVERNMENTAL EXAMPLE

In one South Asian country, the research director of the government's Women's Division initiated a series of actions to ensure that the recommendations contained in *FLS* would be implemented following the conference. She developed a three-pronged strategy: (1) extracting relevant paragraphs of the document and sending them to the appropriate government ministries with a recommendation to take immediate action; (2) organizing networking sessions between NGOs, parliamentarians, experts, and academics about implementation issues; (3) synthesizing available research on women within a policy context to guide programme development. Additionally, each ministry was asked to provide advice on how to integrate *FLS* into their own work.

▶ A NON-GOVERNMENTAL EXAMPLE

In North America, a group of women formed the Women in Dialogue project to use *FLS* as a blueprint for examining the local situation. They formed local committees to undertake research on the situation of women in specific communities. They followed this by convening dialogues in which the researchers would present their findings and then talk about how their findings about women's lives related to the document that emerged from the World Conference. Using *FLS* as a model, the women worked together to write their own forward-looking strategies related to women's lives and issues in the community.

Whether you attend a UN world conference or not, the resolutions and recommendations contained in the final document can be used as a local organizing tool. Here are some suggestions on how to follow-up on the issues raised and decisions of the conference:

- ▶ Order the complete, official version of any final documents from the Conference Secretariat.

- ▶ Identify the appropriate department(s) in your government responsible for implementing and reporting on the outcomes of the conference.

- ▶ Continue to work with international networks. Organizations in countries and regions around the world develop projects and programmes following up on initiatives discussed at UN world conferences.

The process begun in convening a UN world conference does not end with the negotiation of the final document. The work continues into implementation and monitoring.

4

# ANNEX 1:
# SOURCES OF INFORMATION ABOUT THE
# FOURTH UN WORLD CONFERENCE ON WOMEN
▲▲▲▲

▶ United Nations Department of Public Information,
United Nations Headquarters, New York, NY 10017, USA

▶ United Nations Division for the Advancement of Women,
Department for Policy Coordination and Sustainable
Development, 2 UN Plaza, New York, NY 10017, USA

▶ United Nations Non-Governmental Liaison Service,
Palais des Nations, CH-1211 Geneva 10, Switzerland

▶ United Nations Non-Governmental Liaison Service,
866 UN Plaza A-6015, New York, NY 10017, USA

▶ United Nations Development Fund for Women,
304 East 45th Street, 6th Floor, New York, NY 10017, USA

▶ International Institute for Training and Research
for the Advancement of Women,
PO Box 21747, Santo Domingo, Dominican Republic

# ANNEX 2:
## REGIONAL ECONOMIC COMMISSIONS
▲▲▲▲

▶Economic Commission for Africa (ECA)
Africa Hall
P.O. Box 3001
Addis Ababa, Ethiopia
Tel: 251 51 72 00 / Telex: 21029

▶Economic and Social Commission for Asia and
the Pacific (ESCAP)
UN Building, Rajadamnern Ave.
Bangkok, Thailand
Tel: 282 9161 or 282 9200 / Fax: 282 9602

▶Economic Commission for Europe (ECE)*
Palais des Nations
1211 Geneva 10, Switzerland
Tel: 22 917 2893 / Fax: 22 917 0036

▶Economic Commission for Latin America and
the Caribbean (ECLAC)
Avenida Dag Hammarskjold
P.O. Box 179-D
Santiago, Chile
Tel: 208 5051 / 61 Fax: 208 0252

▶Economic and Social Commission for Western Asia
(ESCWA)
Plaza Hotel
P.O. Box 950629
Amman, Jordan
Tel: 962 669 4351 / Fax: 962 266 694981 or 694982

*The ECE region includes the United States and Canada.

# ANNEX 3:
# A SAMPLE UN RESOLUTION ON
# NGO PARTICIPATION
▲▲▲▲

Below is an example of an annex to a UN resolution governing participation of NGOs in a UN world conference.

▲▲▲

**Participation of non-governmental organizations in the Fourth World Conference on Women and its preparatory body**

Non-governmental organizations in consultative status with the Economic and Social Council that express the wish to attend the Conference and the meetings of the Commission on the Status of Women, acting as its preparatory body, will be accredited for participation. Others wishing to be accredited may apply to the Conference Secretariat for this purpose in accordance with the following requirements:

(a) The secretariat of the Fourth World Conference on Women will be responsible for the receipt and preliminary evaluation, in accordance with the provisions given below, of requests from non-governmental organizations for accreditation to the Conference and the Commission on the Status of Women when it is acting as the preparatory body;

(b) All such applications must be accompanied by information on the competence of the organization and on its relevance to the work of the preparatory body, indicating the particular areas of the Conference preparations to which such competence and relevance pertain, and should include the following:

(i) Purposes of the organization

(ii) Information on its programme and activities in areas relevant to the Conference and on the country or countries in which those programmes and activities are carried out

(iii) Confirmation of its activities at the national and/or the international level

(iv) Copies of its annual reports with financial statements and a list of members of the governing body and their country of nationality

(v) A description of its membership, indicating the total number of members of the governing body and their country of nationality.

(c) Non-governmental organizations seeking accreditation will be asked to confirm their interest in the goals and objectives of the Conference;

(d) In cases where the Conference Secretariat believes, on the basis of the information provided in accordance with the present document, that an organization has established its competence and relevance to the work of the Commission on the Status of Women acting as preparatory body, it will recommend to the Commission on the Status of Women that the organization be accredited. In cases where the Conference Secretariat does not recommend the granting of accreditation, it will make such information available to members of the Commission at least one week prior to the start of each session;

(e) The Commission on the Status of Women will decide on all proposals for accreditation within twenty-four hours of the Conference Secretariat's recommendations, having been taken up by the Commission in plenary session. Should a decision not be taken within that period, interim accreditation will be accorded until such time as a decision is taken;

(f) A non-governmental organization that has been granted accreditation to attend one session of the Commission on the Status of Women acting as preparatory body may attend all future sessions and the World Conference;

(g) In recognition of the intergovernmental nature of the Fourth World Conference on Women, non-governmental organizations have no negotiating role in the work of the Conference and its preparatory process;

(h) Relevant non-governmental organizations in consultative status with the Economic and Social Council may be given the opportunity briefly to address the Commission on the Status of Women acting as preparatory body in the plenary meeting and its subsidiary bodies. Other relevant non-governmental organizations may also ask to speak briefly at such meetings. If the number of requests is too large, the Commission will request that non-governmental organizations form themselves into constituencies, with each constituency speaking through one spokesperson. Any oral intervention by a non-governmental organization should, in accordance with normal United Nations practice, be made at the discretion of the Chairman and with the consent of the Commission;

(i) Relevant non-governmental organizations may, at their own expense, make written presentations in the official languages of the United Nations during the preparatory process, as they deem appropriate. Those written presentations will not be issued as official documents unless they are in accordance with the rules of procedure of the Conference.

*Adopted by UN GA on 20 December 1993*

# ANNEX 4:
# HANDBOOK GLOSSARY
▲▲▲▲

**Accreditation**

A formal registration process that enables representatives of non-governmental organizations to attend UN meetings and conferences and their preparatory processes. In order to become accredited to attend a UN world conference and its Preparatory Committee meetings, NGOs which are not in consultative status with the Economic and Social Council must submit specific information about the organization and its work programme.

**AGENDA 21**

*Agenda 21* is the Programme of Action adopted at the 1992 UN Conference on Environment and Development. It contains recommendations for achieving sustainable development in a broad range of areas.

**CSW**

The Commission on the Status of Women (CSW) is a standing specialized subsidiary body of the Economic and Social Council charged with specific functions concerning the advancement of women. Established in 1946, the CSW has served as the preparatory body for each UN world conference on Women. Since 1985, much of its work has focused on monitoring the implementation of *Nairobi Forward-Looking Strategies for the Advancement of Women to the year 2000 (FLS)*.

**Consensus**

Consensus enables resolutions, decisions, or final conference documents to be adopted without a vote. Consensus is achieved through negotiation and compromise and implies agreement among all government delegations.

**Convention**

A convention is a binding international formal agreement among Member States. Ratification indicates that a nation considers itself legally bound by that convention.

**Delegation**

A delegation consists of representatives of a government at a UN conference or meeting. A delegation can include high-level representatives of relevant ministries, technical experts, representatives from the mission or embassy where the conference is held, and, increasingly, NGO representatives.

**ECOSOC**  The Economic and Social Council (ECOSOC) is one of the principal organs of the United Nations set up by the UN Charter. ECOSOC consists of 54 Members of the United Nations elected by Member States for a three-year term. It coordinates the economic and social activities of the UN system.

**Expert Group**  Expert group meetings may be convened by the Conference Secretariat and/or mandated by Member States as part of the preparatory process for a UN world conference to address one of its issues or themes. Experts include academics, representatives of governments and NGOs.

**General Assembly**  The General Assembly is the highest principal organ of the United Nations and consists of all Member States. It governs the work of the United Nations and formally adopts the documents resulting from UN world conferences.

**Group of 77**  The Group of 77 (G-77) is an intergovernmental group established in 1964 to represent the interests of developing countries in the United Nations. The G-77 is named for the 77 developing countries then within the UN system. Today it consists of 132 Member States.

**Member States**  National governments that are members of the United Nations. Currently there are over 180 Member States.

**Non-papers**  Non-papers are prepared for informal consultations among Member States. They serve as a tool to advance the process of reaching consensus. Non-papers are not included in the official record of the conference or meeting.

**PrepCom**  The Preparatory Committee (PrepCom) for a conference is made up of Member States. It holds a series of meetings in preparation for a conference to develop an agenda and a programme of work, and undertakes negotiations on the outcome of the UN world conference.

**Programme of Action**  The Programme of Action is an agreed-upon set of strategies and measures, often accompanied by a Declaration, to achieve the goals of the conference. Member States begin drafting the Programme of Action at PrepCom meetings.

**Rapporteur**  The rapporteur is the officer of a meeting or conference specifically charged with keeping the minutes and writing the report of
each session of the conference.

**Regional Economic**  The Regional Economic Commissions are the standing special-
**Commissions**  ized subsidiary bodies of ECOSOC charged with responsibility
for addressing the concerns of the various world regions.

**Resolution**  A document sponsored by a government or group of governments
that contains a set of recommended actions. Resolutions include
an introductory section – a preamble – outlining the purpose
of the resolution and listing previous decisions adopted on the
subject. The operative part of a resolution specifies the recommended action to be taken.

**Secretariat**  The Secretariat is the body created by the Charter of the United
Nations that consists of international civil servants who work for
the United Nations and carry out its functions.